Mosaics

SABINA ROBBA

MINI · WORKBOOK · SERIES

MEREHURST

CONTENTS

Kitchen splashback (top), floor inset (far left) and birdbath (left)

Tools and materials

Mosaics can be purely decorative or entirely functional works of art. They are created by piecing together small tiles, stones, broken crockery or pottery to create a design. The mosaic technique is not difficult to master, and it requires only a few basic tools and materials.

TOOLS AND EQUIPMENT

There are no set rules as to what tools you should use, but most of what you need can be found in hardware stores and tile suppliers, or look around the home for items that may be useful.

The tools needed to make the mosaic projects are listed with each project and are illustrated on page 63. These and other equipment that you may find useful are listed below.

TILE NIPPERS

There are several methods of cutting tiles but the easiest is to use a pair of tile nippers. Tile nippers are the most versatile tool in a mosaicist's tool kit and are the only major investment you will need to make.

Tile nippers are available in various sizes and usually differ in quality and price. Tungsten carbide-tipped nippers are a worthwhile investment. Make sure the handles are spring-actioned and try them out first by holding them in your hand to see if they feel comfortable.

All of the tesserae used to make the projects in this book were cut using tile nippers.

SETTING UP THE STUDIO

Whether you have a small studio or are intending to work on the kitchen table, you need to make some plans and preparations before you start work.

• Consider the size of the area you are working in and the scale of the project you are intending to tackle.

• If you do not have a studio, organise space on a shelf or in a cupboard to store your equipment.

• Mosaic work can be messy, so cover the table and floor with plastic, old sheets, or anything that can be discarded or washed. Small shards of tiles can be vacuumed up, but when grout dries on carpet or wooden floors it is difficult to remove.

• Make sure you have easy access to water. When grouting and cleaning the mosaic, you will need frequent changes of water.

• If working indoors, ensure that you have plenty of light and fresh air. Find a comfortable chair and work at a steady, leisurely pace.

Plan your work space carefully. Have plenty of fresh air, light and a large work bench on which to spread out your materials.

RUBBER SQUEEGEE

A rubber squeegee is used to spread the grout into the gaps between the tesserae and to wipe off the excess grout. If you do not want to purchase a rubber squeegee, spread the grout with a trowel or palette knife or, wearing rubber gloves, use your hands to spread the grout over the surface, pushing it into all the cracks.

PALETTE KNIFE OR TROWEL

Use a palette knife to spread the tile adhesive directly on the surface or on the back of individual tesserae. A trowel is useful when working on large areas.

SPONGES AND RAGS

These are used to wipe off excess grout from the surface of the mosaic and to polish the finished mosaic.

CONTAINERS

Save plastic or ice cream containers and use them for mixing adhesive and grout. Use glass jars or plastic containers to store your tesserae and other mosaic odds and ends.

SAFETY EQUIPMENT

When working with mosaics you will need rubber gloves, safety goggles and a filter mask (see the box above for further details).

MISCELLANEOUS

For drawing designs you will need paper, ruler and a pencil. If choosing your own colour scheme, coloured pencils or watercolours are useful.

SAFETY

Consider the need for safety when working with mosaics.

- When cutting tiles, even if you only need to cut one or two, always protect your eyes with goggles or glasses. As tiles have a tendency to shatter, wear goggles and cut the tiles at arms' length to prevent small shards flying up into your face.
- When cutting tiles, wear a mask to prevent the inhalation of dust or glass particles.
- Wear rubber gloves when working with cement or grout, and wear a dust mask when polishing off dry grout or when using solvents.

Transfer designs on to the surface using carbon paper and a stylus (or blunt pencil). Carbon paper is available in sheets and one side is coated in carbon. It is usually black or blue, but buy white if you want to transfer a design on to a dark surface.

A felt-tipped pen is useful for outlining pencilled designs for better visibility, and for marking on tiles.

Use a compass for drawing circles and a protractor for measuring angles.

MATERIALS

There is a large range of materials that can be used in a mosaic, ranging from glass tiles to ordinary household china. The following is a list of materials commonly used. This list covers the materials used for the

Where possible, keep your tesserae and other materials stored in glass or plastic jars to help you quickly locate the colour or pattern you need.

projects in this book, but do not let this restrict you. Experiment with different elements and textures to give your mosaic an individual touch.

TESSERAE

These are the small pieces of material that are built up to form the mosaic. There is a large range of materials that are suitable for use in mosaics.

• Glass mosaic tesserae are small squares of coloured glass. Usually smooth on the front, they are slightly ridged on the back, which aids adhesion. They are often used in swimming pools and are popular for bathroom floors and walls. They can be used whole for borders and are easily cut and shaped with tile nippers for more intricate designs.

Glass tesserae are widely available and come in a large range of colours and styles. Prices range according to colour, quality and supplier. It is usual to buy them in sheets, but some of the more expensive colours, such as gold and silver, can be purchased individually (be prepared to pay handsomely for these).

• Ceramic tesserae are available in a matte finish in a range of earthy colours, usually black, white terracotta and brown. They give a flat surface and are hard wearing. Ceramic tesserae can be bought loose or in sheets. A range of both types of tesserae is available from specialist mosaic suppliers.

• Ceramic tiles are sold widely for household use, and range from colourful to plain, through to bright, hand-painted designs. They are available in many different shapes and sizes, which makes them ideal for covering large areas quickly.

Ceramic tiles can be both glazed and unglazed. Unglazed tiles are well suited to designs that have a natural, earthy colour, but they can also be used to provide contrast within a highly colourful, 'glossy' mosaic.

Look out for discontinued lines at tiling suppliers and do not discount tiles that may look a little too bright or old-fashioned: once cut into tesserae and used in small areas, they can take on a whole new life.

• Unusual and colourful old china cups and plates add life to a mosaic. They add interest and detail, and provide a contrast with plainer tiles. Raised patterns, or even the handles from tea cups or coffee mugs, can be incorporated into your design to give it a three-dimensional effect.

You need a little more patience to locate the right piece of china for your mosaic, but second-hand shops or garage sales are great places to start. Another good source is from friends and family: ask them to save their broken plates or cups for you.

• Pebbles and stones can look very effective in a mosaic. Collect them from the beach or river bank and try to select ones that are similar in size.

Marble, slate and granite are also suitable stones for mosaic work.

• Also used in small quantities in this book are coloured glass, mirror, glass beads and pieces of terracotta pots; you can use just about anything that sparks your imagination.

BASES

There are many surfaces suitable for mosaic work, but make sure you choose a base for your mosaic according to where you are planning to use it. A high grade plywood or medium density fibreboard (MDF) are suitable for most projects as they are strong and warp-resistant. If the wood is likely to come into contact with water, seal it before starting the project to prevent moisture entering the wood, causing the adhesive to fail and the wood to warp. Some mosaicists prefer to seal all types of wood before use.

Where the mosaic is likely to come into contact with constant damp or wet, such as in the bathroom or behind the kitchen sink, a waterproof base, such as marine plywood or a pre-sealed board, is needed. Both types of board can be purchased from hardware stores, builders' merchants and timber yards. Ask them to cut the board to size.

If working on a previously painted surface, sand the surface lightly before use. This provides a 'tooth' for the adhesive. Porous surfaces, such as terracotta, should be sealed before use.

ADHESIVES

A quality adhesive is essential to any mosaic work. There are many types to choose from and new products are launched frequently, but there is no strict rule as to what you should use.

If in doubt, talk with your hardware or tile supplier to ensure you make a suitable choice.

Adhesives are broken into two main groups: latex-based multi-purpose and cement-based adhesives. Both types are used to complete the projects in this book.

• Multi-purpose tile adhesive is a two-part adhesive designed to withstand movement and provides great strength. It bonds exceptionally well, is easy to work, and is suitable for many mosaic applications. When cured, the adhesive is completely unaffected by water.

Most of the projects in this book use this adhesive. It is purchased in two parts: a liquid and a rubbery powder. Mix the two parts together just before use, following the manufacturer's instructions. This adhesive is usually sold in bulk quantities, mainly for commercial use, but there are some water-resistant adhesives that are sold in pre-mixed tubs, which are ideal for smaller jobs.

• Cement-based tile adhesive is waterproof, long-lasting and bonds very well with the porous surfaces of terracotta and cement (this is the adhesive used for swimming pools).

The birdbath and garden pot projects use this adhesive. As these surfaces are in frequent, if not constant, contact with water, a high grade cement-based adhesive, such as this, should be used.

• Wallpaper paste is used to temporarily bond tesserae to craft

---

paper when the indirect mosaic method is used (see pages 13–14).

GROUT

Grout is the paste used to fill the gaps, or interstices, between tesserae. It strengthens the mosaic and gives the surface a less jagged finish. Grout is commonly sold as white or grey, but a reasonably extensive range of coloured grouts is available at most hardware stores.

Take your time when choosing a grout colour as this is essential to complement the finished design. As a general guide:

• If you want a bold, well-defined mosaic, choose a grout colour dissimilar to any of the tesserae. This will bring out strong contrasts within the design.

• For a softer, unified design, aim for a grout in a similar tonal range to the mosaic elements.

• When you are not sure what colour grout to use, grey is always a safe, neutral option.

• Plain cement can also be used as a grouting medium.

Basic techniques

Mosaic work can look quite complicated, but the technique is not difficult to master. You do not necessarily need artistic ability or any special skills to achieve great results—just imagination and patience. Each project has step-by-step instructions to guide you, but you may need to refer back to this chapter for more detail.

DECIDING ON DESIGN AND COLOUR

1 A good mosaic starts with design and colour, so take the time to plan this carefully. A pattern or diagram (for the less complicated designs) has been provided for all the projects in this book. You do not need to follow the designs exactly: use them as a source of inspiration for your own design.

2 Each project (except the fruit bowl and bathroom splashback, which use a large range of colours) lists the colours of mosaic materials needed, but this is intended as a guide only. Feel free to choose your own colour scheme but, if you do, make a colour rough of the design first.

3 Once you have decided on design and colour, write a list of the tiles or other mosaic materials that you need. As a guide, indicate the colours you will need more of, and those colours that are used sparingly. Take this with you to the tile shop and use it as a guide when selecting your tiles. You may also want to take this book with you as a handy reference.

DRAWING THE DESIGNS

4 You can draw up your design in many ways:

• If you feel confident, use a pencil and ruler to draw the design, following the diagram or pattern as a guide. You can either draw directly on to the surface, or on to a piece of paper and transfer the design when it is completed.

• If you have access to a photocopier that has an enlarging function, this is a great way to scale up a design. Enlarge the pattern to the size as shown, or if you want a different size, work out the percentage yourself. To do this, divide the intended finished length by the current length and multiply by 100. To capture the entire image you may need to take several photocopies at different points along the design and tape them together.

• Likewise, a design can be planned out on a computer and then printed out to scale.

5 If you are photocopying or drawing the design on paper, transfer it on to the surface using carbon paper. Place the carbon face down on the surface

The range of materials available to the mosaic artist is virtually unlimited. Choose from shells, stones, glass or ceramic mosaic tesserae, tiles, pieces of coloured glass, mirror, beads or broken crockery.

and position the design on top. Use a blunt pencil or stylus to trace around the design.

CUTTING THE TILES

6 Always prepare enough tiles to start work on one area or colour. With larger projects, it may not be convenient to cut all your tiles at once: cut them in batches as you work. Ensure you are wearing the necessary safety equipment (see the box on page 6).

7 A little time is needed to practise cutting or snipping the tiles so, before beginning your project, try cutting a few tiles to form various shapes. For better leverage, hold the handles of the tile nippers as close as possible to the end. Hold the tile in the other hand.

8 To cut a tile in half, angle the tile nippers just on the edge of the tile (in the middle) and squeeze the legs of the nippers together, applying a firm, even pressure. The tile will break in half. Repeat this process to cut the tile into quarters, if necessary.

CUTTING LARGER TILES

• To cut larger tiles into tesserae, it is best to roughly break up the tile first. Place the tile between two soft cloths and strike it with a hammer to break it up into smaller pieces. From this stage, use tile nippers to cut the tesserae to the required shapes.

• Larger items of crockery, such as plates or saucers, can also be broken up this way, or you can drop them on the floor or table (this can be quite enjoyable—every mosaic artist should try this at least once). Use tile nippers to shape the broken pieces.

9 To cut tiles into circles or petal shapes, cut off the four corners and use the outer edge of the tile nippers to nibble the tile. Slowly work around the tile to achieve the desired shape. You may prefer to use a felt-tipped pen and draw the shape on to the tile first but, with practice, you will find that this is not necessary. Several cuts may be required to achieve a specific shape.

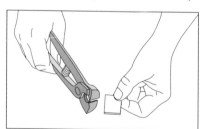

7 Before you begin work on the mosaic, practise holding the tile nippers and cutting tiles.

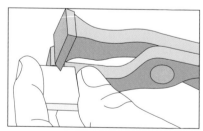

8 To cut the tile in half, angle the tile nippers on the edge of the tile and squeeze the nippers together.

10 To cut a tile to fit an exact shape, hold the tile over the gap in the mosaic, draw a line on the tile to indicate the area that needs to be cut, and cut it out. As you gain confidence you will be able to do this without drawing on the tile.

LAYING THE TESSERAE

11 Choose a suitable adhesive for your project (if in doubt, enquire at your local hardware store) and apply it to the surface, working on a small area at a time. Use a palette knife or small trowel to do this. Alternatively, 'butter' the back of the tesserae and stick on to the surface, one at a time (this is the preferred method when you do not want the adhesive to obscure the outline of your design).

12 There are two methods of laying the tesserae and these are commonly referred to as the 'direct' and 'indirect' methods. These are the only two techniques you need to complete all the projects in this book.
• The direct method is the easiest of the two methods. The tiles are cut and the tesserae are stuck directly on

THE DIRECT OR THE INDIRECT METHOD?

The size and shape of your mosaic will determine which method you should use to complete it.

The direct method is usually recommended for the following:
• mosaic murals, splashbacks and designs that use a lot of colour;
• work on surfaces that are uneven or three-dimensional.

The disadvantage of the direct method is if you are using various types of tesserae, the uneven thickness of the tesserae will give you an uneven finished surface.

The indirect method is recommended for:
• work that cannot be carried out directly on site;
• mosaics that require the finished surface to be perfectly flat, such as a floor mosaic;
• work on a detailed design that would otherwise be partly obscured by the adhesive when applying the direct method.

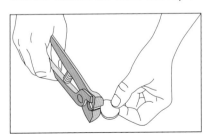

9 To cut tiles into circles or petal shapes, use the outer edge of the tile nippers to nibble the tile.

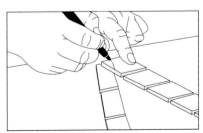

10 To cut a tile to fit an exact shape, hold the tile over the gap and draw a line where it needs to be cut.

to the surface. This is also the most rewarding form of mosaic as you can watch the mosaic grow before your eyes. All the projects in this book, with the exception of the floor inset, are made using this method.

• The indirect method requires a little more time in execution.

Draw the design on brown paper and paste the tesserae on it upside down using a temporary adhesive—a water-based glue, such as wallpaper paste, is ideal. When the mosaic is completed (in this temporary state) transfer it to its permanent base. If the design is large, you may need to ask someone to help you with this (or work the mosaic in smaller sections and then transfer the pieces).

Place the tiles on the permanent base on a bed of adhesive, with the paper facing up. Allow 24 hours for the adhesive to set. Using a cloth and warm water, wipe over the mosaic to break the bond of the wallpaper paste; peel away the paper to reveal the mosaic.

The instructions for the indirect method are explained on pages 55–7.

COLOURED GROUT

If you are adding colour to powdered grout, make sure that you mix enough grout to complete the entire project. Unless you make careful measurements when adding the powdered colour it will be difficult to achieve exactly the same colour each time.

HINT

Grout will spread easier if the surface is slightly damp.

GROUTING

13 Grouting is the method of rubbing cement mortar into the gaps between the tesserae, making the surface less jagged. Grout gives strength and durability to the mosaic.

To mix the grout, place the powder in a bucket or mixing container, make a well in the centre and slowly add the water, mixing the powder into the water. Make sure there are no lumps and the mixture is fairly dry; not wet. If you want to add colour to a white grout, do so before adding any water. Mix up enough grout to cover the entire mosaic: more grout is always better than too little (see the box on coloured grout, below left).

14 Wearing rubber gloves and using a squeegee, evenly spread the grout on to the mosaic. Press firmly to ensure the grout fills all the gaps. If you do not have a squeegee, use a

13 Place the grout powder in a bowl, make a well in the centre and slowly add the water.

trowel or spatula to spread the grout. On smaller or uneven surfaces, you may find it easier to use your hands to spread the grout (put on a pair of rubber gloves first).

15 Remove the excess grout using either the rubber squeegee, a spatula or a cloth. Allow the mosaic to stand for 5–10 minutes.

16 With a damp sponge, wipe over the surface to reveal the mosaic. Rinse the sponge out regularly.

17 Once the mosaic is completely dry, a light film of cement powder will appear. Use a combination of slightly damp and dry rags to polish the completed project.

HANGING THE MOSAIC

18 Deciding where and how to hang your mosaic (if this is necessary) may be the last step, but you should think about this before you start work.

Usually, a screw inserted through the corners of the sheeting or board and into the wall is strong enough to support the weight of the mosaic (make sure your walls and the screws are strong enough to hold the weight). This method is quite permanent, but the board can be removed if necessary.

In order to hide the screws from view, leave a tessera off each corner of the sheeting. Attach the design to the wall with screws, and then fix the remaining tesserae over the screws to hide them. Grout the area.

CLEANING MOSAICS

It may be necessary to use a commercial tile cleaner or a diluted solution of hydrochloric acid to give your mosaic its final clean. This may be the case if you are using a cement-based adhesive, or if the grout has dried too much and it is difficult to remove it with soap and water. If the surface film of grout cannot be removed with a cloth and water try the following method using dilute hydrochloric acid.

1 If possible, take the mosaic outside to be cleaned. Wear gloves and eye protection at all times when handling the hydrochloric acid. If there are any splashes, wash the area immediately with lots of water.

2 Add one part acid to fifteen parts of water in a bucket or container. Always add the acid to the water to minimise the chance of the acid splashing up and burning you.

3 Brush the acid solution over the mosaic and immediately wash it off with lots of clean water. It is important that no trace of acid be left on the mosaic.

4 Finally, allow the surface to dry, and then polish the mosaic with a soft cloth.

This project is completed using the direct method of applying mosaics in which the tesserae are cut and glued directly on the surface. The black grout helps to emphasise the brightly coloured design.

Trivet

A simple geometrical design makes this trivet the perfect project for beginners to mosaic. The design is easy to follow and little or no cutting is required, as the tesserae are either laid whole or cut in half.

TOOLS	MATERIALS
• Brushes for sealer and paint	• Water-based sealer
• Pencil	• 260 x 260 mm plywood (18 mm thick)
• Ruler	• 20 x 20 mm glass mosaic tesserae: orange, light blue, beige, blue
• Mixing containers	
• Palette knife	• 25 x 25 mm glass mosaic tesserae: red, blue
• Goggles and mask	
• Tile nippers	• Multi-purpose tile adhesive
• Rubber gloves	• Black grout
• Rubber squeegee	• Black paint
• Rags or cloths	• Rubber buffers or felt pads (optional)
• Sponges	

PREPARATION

1 Using the brush, apply one coat of water-based sealer to the plywood square. If the trivet is to be used as a stand for a kettle, or if it will need to be cleaned regularly, it will come into contact with water and should be sealed. The sealer will prevent moisture entering the wood, which may cause it to swell and buckle. Allow the sealer to dry thoroughly.

2 Using a pencil and ruler, draw the design on to the plywood square, following the diagram on page 19. You do not need to draw the design in full detail, such as the individual positions for each tesserae, you only need a basic guide for your mosaic. When drawing up the design, note that the tesserae are spaced apart (except for the central square) to allow room for the grout.

ALTERNATIVES

Do not restrict yourself to using one design for one project. This trivet is useful as a resting place for hot pots or kettles, but you can use the same design on thinner pieces of plywood to make a set of place mats, or alter to suit the frame of a mirror.

3 Without using any adhesive, place a row of uncut orange and light blue tesserae along the first row of the central square. Position the tesserae as closely together as possible. If they do not fit, adjust your drawn lines.

FIXING THE TESSERAE

4 Using a palette knife, apply tile adhesive to the square. Stick the orange and light blue tesserae on the adhesive, alternating the two colours. Work in rows to complete the square.

5 Apply adhesive to the four corners of the board and stick a large red mosaic tessera on each corner. You can also use the palette knife to spread the adhesive on the back of the tiles. This process is called 'buttering'.

6 Wearing goggles, cut the larger blue tesserae in half using tile nippers.

7 Butter the back of each blue tessera, and stick them between the red corners to form a border around the trivet. Fourteen half tesserae are used on each side. Leave a 2–3 mm gap between the tesserae.

8 Cut the beige tesserae in half. Butter them with adhesive and place them between the blue border and the central square. To neaten the row, place the tesserae so that the cut edge faces the blue border. Allow the adhesive to set for 1–2 hours.

9 Rest the trivet on its edge and fix the smaller whole blue tesserae along one side. Allow the adhesive to set. Turn the trivet and repeat this process to complete all four sides. Allow 24 hours for the adhesive to dry before grouting.

FINISHING

10 Wearing rubber gloves and a mask and using the rubber squeegee, apply the black grout over the surface (see Grouting, pages 14–15). Use your fingers to push the grout into areas that you may have missed. If you do not have a squeegee, use your hands or a palette knife to spread the grout over the surface.

11 Wipe off the excess grout with the squeegee or a rag; allow the mosaic to stand for 5–10 minutes.

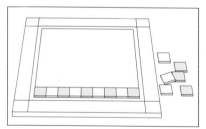

3 To check the tesserae fit the design, position a row of orange and light blue tesserae inside the central square.

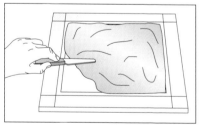

4 Using a palette knife, apply a thick layer of tile adhesive to the central area of the trivet.

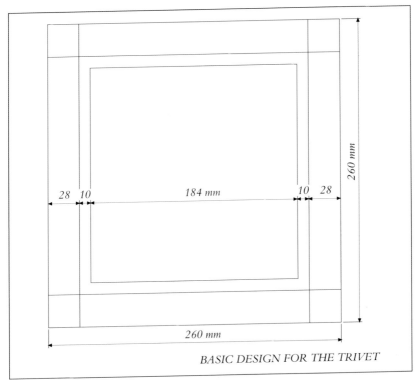

28 | 10 | 184 mm | 10 | 28

260 mm

260 mm

BASIC DESIGN FOR THE TRIVET

12 Using a damp sponge, wipe over the mosaic to remove any grout residue. When it is completely dry, a light film of cement powder will appear. Alternate slightly damp and dry rags to polish the trivet.

13 Paint the back of the trivet with black paint to protect the plywood. Add rubber buffers or felt pads to the plywood to raise the trivet slightly. This will prevent it from scratching the table top or kitchen bench.

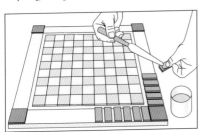

7 Butter the back of the blue tesserae with adhesive and place them around the edge of the trivet.

10 Using the rubber squeegee and wearing gloves to protect your hands, spread the grout over the surface.

Whatever colours you choose for this mosaic, make sure there is a contrast between the background colour and the numbers. If the colours are too similar, it will be difficult to read the number from a distance.

House number

Create a warm welcome to your home with this simple mosaic. The design is suitable for beginners, but more detailed cutting is required to make up the numbers. The mosaic is made up of glass mosaic tiles and broken china.

TOOLS

- Brushes for sealer and paint
- Pencil and ruler
- Stylus (optional)
- Goggles and mask
- Tile nippers
- Mixing containers
- Palette knife
- Rubber gloves
- Rubber squeegee
- Rags or cloths
- Sponges

MATERIALS

- 300 x 220 mm plywood (18 mm thick)
- Exterior water-based sealer
- Carbon paper (optional)
- Tracing paper (optional)
- 20 x 20 mm glass mosaic tesserae: cream
- 20 x 20 mm glass mosaic tesserae: bronze, green
- Small amount of patterned china
- Multi-purpose tile adhesive
- Black grout
- Black paint
- Fastening plate or screws

PREPARATION

1 If the house number will be exposed to the elements, seal the wood to prevent water seeping in and causing the panel to buckle. Apply two coats of the sealer and allow 24 hours for it to dry between each coat (or according to the manufacturer's instructions for the product you are using).

2 Following the basic diagram on page 23, draw the design on to the plywood, using a ruler to ensure all lines are straight (vary the size of the panel depending on how many numbers you need to fit on it). Add in the numbers for your house in freehand. If preferred, practise drawing the numbers on paper first (so you can easily rub out any

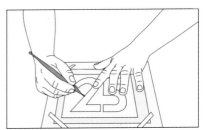

2 Using tracing paper and carbon paper, transfer the numbers for your house on to the centre of the board.

The house number requires more accurate tile cutting, so take your time when doing this.

mistakes) and then use carbon paper, tracing paper and a stylus to transfer the numbers to the centre of the board. If preferred, and if your house number will be positioned a long way from the street, increase the size of the numbers for better visibility.

3 Wearing a mask and goggles to protect your eyes, use the tile nippers to cut the tesserae to fit the design.
• The cream tesserae are used whole, and are also cut into smaller square or rectangular shapes to make up the background.
• The bronze tesserae are shaped to fit the two numbers, and are also cut into small squares (approximately 10 x 10 mm) to fit around the

chequered border. The green tesserae are used whole around the sides of the panel, and smaller squares are used for the border.
• The patterned china is cut into four squares for the corners of the panel.

FIXING THE TESSERAE

4 Using the palette knife, spread the tile adhesive over a small section of the board. Alternatively, butter the backs of each tessera with the adhesive. It is a good idea to start working in the middle, starting with the number. Work carefully as you fit the tiles into the numbers, ensuring they fit accurately within the drawn lines: you want the number to be clear.

5 Working on small sections at a time, fill in the background using the cream tesserae.

6 Using small squares of bronze and green tesserae, work around the border of the panel, alternating the colours to achieve a chequered effect. Fix the patterned china squares on the four corners.

5 Working on small sections at a time, fill in around the numbers with cream tesserae.

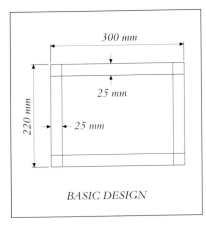

BASIC DESIGN

7 Allow the adhesive to dry for about two hours. Rest the panel on its edge and fix 20 x 20 mm whole green tesserae along one side. Allow the adhesive to set. Turn the panel and repeat this process until all four sides are completed. Before grouting, allow 24 hours for the adhesive to dry thoroughly.

FINISHING

8 Using the rubber squeegee, spread liberal amounts of the black grout over the surface, pushing it into all the cracks. Wipe off the excess with a cloth or rag (see Grouting, pages 14–15). Allow the grout to set for about ten minutes.

9 With a damp sponge, wipe over the surface to reveal the mosaic. Rinse out the sponge regularly as you remove the grout. Once the mosaic is completely dry, a light film of residue grout will be left on the surface—wipe this off with a clean, dry rag.

10 Paint the back of the panel and, when dry, attach a fastening plate or screws. Allow the mosaic to dry for a further 24 hours before hanging it on the wall.

HINT

There is no set order in which you should work your mosaic. Some mosaicists like to start at the bottom and work their way up, and others like to work on one colour or area at a time. The instructions given for all the projects in this book are intended as guidelines: you will find that, with practice, you will develop your own style and routine.

9 Using a damp sponge, wipe over the surface to reveal the mosaic. Rinse the sponge regularly.

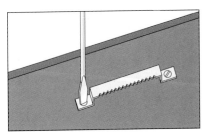

10 Attach a fastening plate or screws to the back of the panel so it can be hung on the wall.

The frame for this mirror was cut by hand, which means you can cut it to fit any area, big or small. If you do not have the necessary cutting tools, ask your local hardware centre to cut the wood for you.

Mirror

Save your broken plates or cups, or beads from old necklaces, and give them a new lease of life as decoration for this mirror. If you do not have any broken crockery lying around, you will be sure to find plenty of cheap and colourful items in second-hand shops or at garage sales.

TOOLS	MATERIALS
• Pencil	• 350 x 350 mm plywood (18 mm thick)
• Ruler	• Coloured glass★: dark blue, light blue
• Drill	• Patterned blue china
• Jigsaw	• Small blue glass beads: 20 long, 20 short
• Router (optional)	• Large, flat beads: dark blue, light blue
• Sharp chisel	• Small amount of gold china
• Goggles and mask	• Large gold beads
• Tile nippers	• Multi-purpose tile adhesive
• Mixing containers	• Yellow grout
• Palette knife	• Yellow paint
• Rubber gloves	• Frame hanger hook
• Sponges	• 160 x 160 mm mirror
• Rags or cloths	• Four small corner clips and screws
• Brush	★ If preferred, substitute ceramic or glass mosaic tesserae for the glass.

PREPARATION

1 To cut out an area for the mirror, use a pencil and ruler and draw a 150 x 150 mm square in the centre of the piece of plywood (or draw the square to fit the size of your mirror).

2 Drill a hole in the centre of the plywood square, large enough for a jigsaw blade to fit in, and use the jigsaw to cut out a square, following the marked lines.

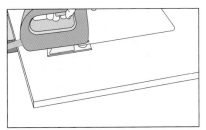

2 Drill a hole in the centre of the square and use the jigsaw to cut out along the marked lines.

3 To create a ledge for the mirror to sit on, run a 5 mm rebate routing bit on the back of the frame, around the inside frame area. Use a sharp chisel to square off the rounded corners. If you do not have a router, draw a line 5 mm in from the internal edge and, with a sharp chisel, remove wood to the depth of 5 mm (or deep enough to accommodate the mirror so it sits flush with the back of the frame).

4 Wearing goggles and a mask, cut the pieces of glass and china into irregularly sized triangular shapes. As it is difficult to estimate how many tesserae you will need, cut enough pieces to start work and then cut more as you need them.

5 Before applying any adhesive, lay out a section of the design on the frame to get an idea of the overall effect. As there are many elements in this design, and to prevent it from looking too mismatched, group the elements around the frame. Generally, larger pieces of dark blue glass are used around the outside edge, the broken china in the centre, and the light blue glass and glass beads around the inside of the frame. Keeping to one or two colours helps to unify the design.

FIXING THE TESSERAE

6 Using the palette knife, apply tile adhesive along one side of the frame and stick the pieces of dark blue glass around the outer border. Complete all four sides in this manner.

BUYING GLASS

The blue coloured glass used for this project was purchased from a supplier of glass windows. You may be able to buy cheap offcuts at some companies.

---

7 Stick the small blue glass beads around the inner edge of the frame, alternating the two sizes of beads. Spread the adhesive in a thin line on one side, stick on the beads, and then start work on the next side. Add a row of small pieces of light blue glass around the beads.

8 Following the main photograph as a guide, add in the two flat beads in the corners of the frame: the four dark blue beads are placed on the outer corners and the light blue beads are placed on the inner corners.

9 Loosely fill in the background with pieces of china or crockery. Use small pieces of gold tesserae (these were from a gold plate) and gold-coloured beads to highlight the design and fill small spaces.

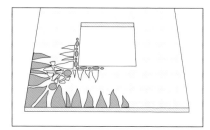

5 Without using any adhesive, lay out a section of the design on the frame to see how it looks.

10 When the surface of the frame is complete, allow the adhesive to set for 1–2 hours.

11 Cut small pieces of glass to be used around the inner and outer edges of the frame. Use rectangular pieces of dark blue glass for the outer edge, and small squares of light blue for the inner edge. Spread the adhesive on one side of the frame at a time and stick the glass tesserae in place. When working on the inner edge, be careful that the glass tesserae do not protrude into the rebated edge, as this is where the mirror will sit. Allow 24 hours for the adhesive to dry thoroughly before grouting.

FINISHING

12 Yellow grout is used here as this colour teams well with the blue tones. As the surface is uneven apply the grout with your hands, wearing rubber gloves (take extra care when doing this or wear two pairs of gloves to protect your hands from being cut on the uneven edges). Apply the grout, ensuring it fills all the gaps (see Grouting, pages 14–15).

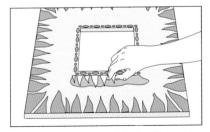

7 Position a row of light blue glass around the glass beads. Work on one side at a time.

HINTS

Mosaic work can hide the surface of ugly or damaged items that might otherwise be thrown away.
●Instead of using a new piece of wood, and cutting it to make the frame, you may have a frame and mirror that you no longer like. As long as the surface of the frame is relatively flat, this will make an ideal base for your mosaic project. If the frame is already painted, lightly sand the surface before you start working on it.
●If you are using a frame with a mirror that cannot be removed, place masking tape or cardboard over the glass to protect it.

13 Wipe off the excess grout with a sponge, rinsing the sponge as you work. You will need to go over the surface several times to ensure all the grout is removed. Allow to dry for 24 hours.

14 When the mosaic is completely dry, a light film of residue grout will be left on the surface—polish this off with a clean, dry rag.

15 Paint the back of the frame to protect the plywood. This frame is painted yellow to match the grout. Add the frame hanger hooks.

16 Insert the mirror into the frame (this mirror has a bevelled edge). Screw in four small corner clips to hold the mirror in place.

Fruit bowl

The saucer of a large terracotta pot serves as the base for this colourful fruit platter. To achieve some degree of realism, you need to choose the colours for your fruit carefully, and take time when cutting the tesserae so they fit accurately within your design.

TOOLS

- Brush
- Pencil
- Stylus (optional)
- Goggles and mask
- Tile nippers
- Mixing containers
- Palette knife
- Rubber gloves
- Rags or cloths
- Sponges

MATERIALS

- Shallow terracotta bowl or large plant pot base (approximately 460 mm in diameter)
- Waterproof sealer
- Tracing paper (optional)
- Carbon paper (optional)
- Glass mosaic tesserae: assorted colours (see steps 4–8)
- Multi-purpose tile adhesive
- Grey grout

PREPARATION

1 Seal the entire terracotta bowl with water-based sealer. As the bowl may need to be wiped, the sealer will prevent water entering the porous terracotta, causing the tile adhesive to weaken. Allow the sealer to dry.

2 Photocopy the pieces of fruit from the pattern on page 58 and enlarge the design as indicated, or to fit the size of your bowl. Transfer the design on to the bowl using carbon paper and a stylus (see pages 10–12). Position the pieces of fruit on the bowl, arranging them as shown. Alternatively, draw the fruit in freehand directly on to the bowl.

3 Wearing goggles, cut tesserae to complete the first piece of fruit. Cut the tesserae as you go, working on one piece of fruit at a time.

FIXING THE TESSERAE

4 Apply the tesserae to the fruit first. Each piece of fruit uses two or more

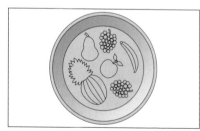

2 Draw the pieces of fruit on to the base of the bowl, or trace and transfer them using the pattern.

28

A clever use of colour and tone are used to create this fruit design. Each piece of fruit uses two or more shades of one colour to give it shape and definition—only one colour for each fruit would leave the design looking rather dull and flat.

Where possible, define the pieces of fruit by outlining them with a single row of thin tesserae. This gives a better flow to the mosaic and neatens the effect.

shades of one colour to build up tone and highlights. For example, the apple is made up mainly from crimson tesserae, but a few brighter red tesserae are placed around the base of the apple to add highlights. Before using adhesive, experiment with the various effects you can achieve by using different shades of the one colour.

5 Using adhesive, complete the fruit using the colours as follows (this is a guide only—feel free to experiment with your own colour choices):

• Grapes: Cut the purple tesserae into small circles. Vary the sizes slightly. Use two tones of purple to mosaic the grapes. Add a brown stem.

• Banana: This fruit is worked using one shade of yellow. Long, thin black tesserae are used down the middle of the banana, and small black squares are placed at the top and bottom.

• Apple: Outline the apple with thin crimson tesserae, and fill in the centre. Highlight areas of the apple with bright red. Add a brown stem and two green leaves.

• Pear: Outline the pear with small, thin green tesserae and fill in the centre with two or three shades of green. Add a brown stem.

• Pineapple: The base is made up of five orange/yellow tones. Outline the base with thin brown tesserae, add four vertical lines running down the base, and fill in between with the other colours. Add leaf-like shapes to outline the top of the pineapple using three to four shades of green. Fill in with square-shaped tesserae.

6 Cut thin rectangular orange tesserae to run around the base of the bowl. Fix in place with adhesive.

7 Use a solid, contrasting colour to fill in the base of the bowl. Small pieces of dark blue tesserae are used for this bowl. To keep the mosaic work neat, start by sticking a row of rectangular blue tesserae around the row of orange. Fill in the base using randomly shaped tesserae, working on small areas at a time.

8 Use small rectangles (approximately 18 x 20 mm) of turquoise and dark blue to complete the sides of the bowl. The pattern is made up of five vertical rows of dark blue, and two vertical rows of turquoise, repeated. Mark the positions of these tesserae in pencil around the sides of the bowl, and adjust the spacing so they fit around the circumference without needing to be cut.

9 Using the palette knife, apply the adhesive to the sides of the bowl. Allow it to stand for 10 minutes so it becomes slightly tacky. If the

---

ALTERNATIVE

If you prefer to create an easier design using fewer colours, select one or two pieces of fruit, such as the pear and apple, and repeat these motifs around the bowl.

---

adhesive is too wet, the tesserae will slide down the sides. Position the uncut bevelled edge of the tesserae uppermost for both rows to make the finish neater.

10 Cut thin, rectangular red tesserae to run around the top of the bowl and fix them in place with adhesive. Allow 24 hours to dry.

FINISHING
11 Wearing gloves and using your hands, spread the grout over the tesserae, pushing it into all the gaps between the tesserae (a rubber squeegee may be difficult to manoeuvre within the bowl). Wipe off the excess with a cloth or rag, then use damp sponges to wipe away the residual grout. When dry, polish with a cloth (see Grouting, pages 14–15).

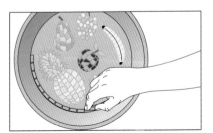

6 Use adhesive to fix a row of thin orange tesserae around the base of the bowl.

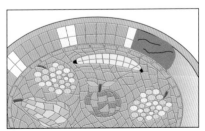

9 Position the tesserae on the sides of the bowl. Place the uncut bevelled edge of the tesserae uppermost.

Non-glazed tesserae, such as these ceramic tiles, add to the rustic appearance of this pot, especially when used with terracotta and pebbles. The design plays a secondary role: the emphasis is on colour and the type of materials used.

Garden pot

This plant pot uses an assortment of pebbles and earth-coloured tesserae to give it a rustic character. Allow yourself plenty of time to complete this project, as each side of the pot must be completed and allowed to dry before beginning on the next.

TOOLS
• Brush
• Goggles and mask
• Tile nippers
• Old towel
• Mixing containers
• Palette knife
• Rubber gloves
• Rags or cloths
• Sponges

MATERIALS
• Terracotta pot (square or hexagonal)
• Water-based sealer
• 24 x 24 mm ceramic tiles in earth colours: brown, black, light grey, yellow, beige
• Small terracotta pot (smashed to make tesserae)
• Assortment of pebbles★
• Cement-based tile adhesive
• Terracotta-coloured grout
★ Larger pebbles, in a variety of colours, are used around the top of the pot and smaller ones, all brown, are used down the sides of the pot.

PREPARATION

1 Seal all surfaces of the pot using a water-based sealer. Ensure the interior of the pot is well sealed: the sealer prevents the moisture seeping through the porous terracotta and weakening the adhesion of the tesserae around the outside of the pot. Allow the sealer to dry.

2 Wearing goggles to protect your eyes and a mask to prevent inhalation of dust particles, prepare enough ceramic tiles to complete at least one side of the pot. The mosaic design for this pot is made up of small squares and thin rectangular tesserae. Smash the terracotta pot and cut it into long, thin rectangles. Without using adhesive, space the large pebbles along one side of the pot to see if you have enough to complete all sides. If not, increase the spacing between the pebbles.

FIXING THE TESSERAE

3 Place an old towel on the work surface and lie the pot on its side. Using the palette knife and the cement-based tile adhesive, apply the adhesive in a thin strip along one side of the pot, just under the rim. This type of adhesive is waterproof and bonds well with the porous surfaces of terracotta.

4 Fix a single row of larger pebbles around the top of the pot, pushing them into the adhesive. Use pebbles that are similar in size to create a uniform effect. If some of the pebbles are too long they will jut into the row below.

5 Remembering to work on one side at a time, spread adhesive along the rim of the pot. Fix a row of brown tesserae to the pot. Similarly, stick a row of thin, rectangular brown tesserae below the pebbles.

6 Starting from the middle of one side, fix a vertical row of small square black tesserae to the pot. On either side of this, fix a row of smaller brown pebbles. If possible, try to use pebbles that are similar in size and shape. Leave enough room at the bottom of the pot for a row of thin brown tesserae.

7 Moving in an outward direction, fix a single row of light grey tesserae on either side of the small pebbles, following the photograph on the right as a guide.

8 Fix two vertical rows of long, thin pieces of terracotta to create a border around the yellow.

9 Continue laying vertical rows of tesserae in this manner until one side of the pot is completed. The size and shape of your pot will determine how many rows of tesserae are needed to complete the mosaic work. If your pot is larger than the one used here, you may want to add in extra rows using different coloured tesserae, or continue to repeat the rows of colours until the side is completed.

10 To complete the design for this side, fix a row of small square-shaped tesserae around the base.

11 Allow the adhesive to dry for about two hours. Turn the pot onto the next side and repeat this process to finish all the sides.

12 To finish laying the tesserae, stand the pot upright and tile around the top of the rim. Use brown tesserae cut into large rectangles and stick them around the top of the pot.

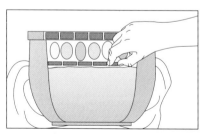

5 Spread some adhesive below the pebbles and fix a row of thin brown tesserae to the pot.

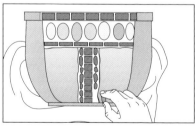

6 Fix a row of small black tesserae down the middle of the pot. Fix a row of pebbles on either side.

A paler grout allows the colour and texture of the materials used in this pot to be the main emphasis.

To fill in the gaps in the corners, cut the brown tesserae into triangular or wedge-shaped pieces and stick them in the corners.

FINISHING

13 Allow 24 hours for the adhesive to dry and then grout. This pot uses a terracotta-coloured grout to complement the earthy elements of

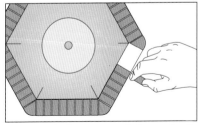

12 Stand the pot upright and tile around the top of the rim using larger rectangular brown tesserae.

CURING TIMES

To allow the mosaic to cure properly, it is best to cover it with a damp cloth and allow it to stand for at least three days before using it.

the pot. As the pot has an uneven surface it is easiest to apply the grout with your hands. Wearing rubber gloves, spread the grout over the surface, pushing it around the pebbles and other mosaic pieces. Wipe off the excess grout with a rag and let it stand for 5–10 minutes.

14 Use a sponge to wipe away the residual grout, rinsing the sponge out in water as you work. You will need to go over the surface several times to clean off the grout. Allow to dry for 24 hours.

15 When the mosaic is completely dry, a light film of grout will be left on the surface—polish this off with a clean, dry rag.

HINTS

Clean up your grouting tools soon after you have finished using them. The wet grout washes off easily in water, but once hardened it is difficult to remove.

If your bucket of water has grout residue in it, never throw the water down the sink as the sand and cement will clog up the drain.

A larger project, such as this table, may take several sittings to complete, but the results can be stunning. Only one type of tile is used (rather than a mix of materials) to ensure the surface is level.

Table top

This table is striking in its bold use of design and colour. The top is cut from a large piece of plywood, and the wrought iron base and legs were especially made by a blacksmith.

TOOLS

- Router
- Brush
- Pencil
- Ruler
- Protractor
- Compass (see the box on page 39)
- Stylus (optional)
- Goggles and mask
- Tile nippers
- Mixing containers
- Palette knife
- Rubber gloves
- Rubber squeegee
- Rags and cloths
- Sponges

MATERIALS

- 25 mm plywood★ 1000 mm in diameter
- Exterior water-based sealer
- Large ceramic floor or wall tiles: red, dark green, orange, lemon-green, light green, cream, mustard, patterned mix for border
- Tracing paper (optional)
- Carbon paper (optional)
- Multi-purpose tile adhesive
- Black grout

★ If the table is intended for outdoor use, a high grade waterproof plywood is recommended.

PREPARATION

1 Using a router, cut out a round piece of plywood measuring 1000 mm in diameter. Alternatively, specialist hardware or timber yards can cut out the table top for you.

2 You may already have a ready-made table with a glass or wooden top that you can use. Remove the glass and insert the piece of plywood in its place. Otherwise, take the wood to a blacksmith and ask for a 30 mm wide metal band to be made to support the table top. You will need twelve small nail holes to be drilled in the centre of the band, spacing them 260 mm apart (the plywood is held in place with nails). Decide on the design of legs for your table.

3 If the table is intended for outdoor use, waterproof the wood using a water-based sealer. Allow it to dry.

DRAWING THE DESIGN

4 Following the diagram on page 38, draw the basic design for the table. Alternatively, use a photocopier to

enlarge the pattern, which is located on page 59. Using carbon paper and the stylus, transfer the design to your table. (If you prefer to mosaic a square table, this design can be adapted to fit. Keep the star in the centre of the design, and following the same measurements given in the diagram below, draw the design using squares instead of circles.)

5 If you are using the diagram to draw the design, first locate the exact centre of the plywood circle and mark

---

DRAWING DESIGNS

Ensure that the pencil lines for your design are clearly visible. You may want to go over them with a felt-tipped pen for better visibility.

---

it with a pencil. Draw a line through this point from one side to the other.

6 Divide the table into eight even 'pie' sections. To do this, place the protractor on the pencil line and mark off three angles of 45 degrees. Place

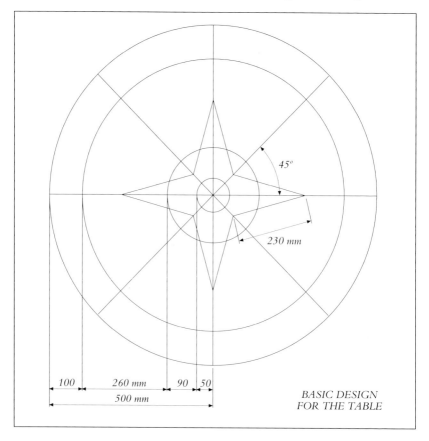

45°

230 mm

100   260 mm   90   50

500 mm

BASIC DESIGN
FOR THE TABLE

DRAWING CIRCLES

If you do not have a compass, you can improvise by using a piece of string, a pencil and a nail.

1 Insert a nail into the centre of the board, then tie a piece of string to the nail.

2 Measure out the string to the length required and tie a loop in the other end. Slip the loop over the pencil.

3 Holding the string taut, draw a circle around the board. Adjust the length of string to draw circles of different sizes.

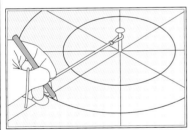

3 Put the pencil through the loop and, holding the string taut, draw a circle around the board.

the protractor on the opposite side and do the same. Rule up the lines following the marked points.

7 Using a compass, draw three circles on the table, using the measurements given on the diagram. If you do not have a compass, use the string and pencil method (see the box above). Draw a star in the centre of the table.

FIXING THE TESSERAE

8 When working on a large table such as this, it is difficult to prepare all the tiles in advance. Wearing goggles, cut enough tiles to complete one area of the table: you can cut more tiles as you need them.

9 Starting in the centre of the table, fill the inner circle with red tesserae cut into eight wedges. Spread the adhesive on to the table with a palette knife and fix the tesserae in place. Surround the wedges with a row of thin, rectangular red tesserae.

10 Using thin, rectangular shaped tesserae, follow the pencilled design to establish outlines for all the geometric elements.

Use dark green for the outer circle, orange for the middle circle (note that the orange circle is not continuous, but is interrupted by the green star and the red radiating lines) and lemon-green for the inner circle. Use red for the eight radiating lines and light green to outline the star (see the diagram on page 40).

Without using adhesive, position all the cut tesserae on the table to ensure that they will fit your pattern. When you are happy with their placement, fix them with the adhesive, working on a section at a time. It may be easier in some areas to butter the backs of the tesserae with the adhesive and press them onto the surface: if you apply the adhesive directly on the table you will obscure your drawn lines.

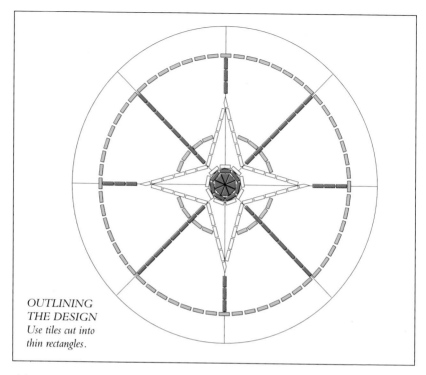

OUTLINING
THE DESIGN
Use tiles cut into
thin rectangles.

11 Using irregularly shaped cream tesserae, fill in the eight large segments between the outer and inner circles. Apply the adhesive directly to the surface, working on small areas at a time, and fix the tesserae in place.

12 Fill the small areas between the middle orange circle and the star with mustard tesserae.

13 Use a mixture of wedge and large rectangular shaped dark green tesserae to complete the star.

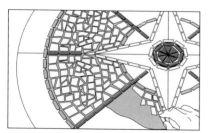

11 Use cream tesserae to fill in the eight segments between the outer and inner circles.

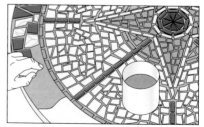

14 Apply the adhesive to one area of the border and fix a mixture of plain and patterned tesserae.

Outline the basic elements of the design, as shown in the diagram on the left, and then fill in the shapes using randomly sized and shaped tesserae.

14 Fill in around the border using a combination of tesserae, plain and patterned, to complete the design.

FINISHING

15 Allow 24 hours for the adhesive to dry before grouting the table. Black grout is used to contrast with the brightly coloured design.

16 Wearing rubber gloves and using the rubber squeegee, apply liberal amounts of the grout over the surface. Use your hands to push the grout into any cracks that you may have missed. Wipe off the excess grout with the squeegee or with a cloth or rag and allow the mosaic to stand for 5–10 minutes (see Grouting, pages 14–15).

17 With a damp sponge, and rinsing regularly, wipe over the surface to reveal the mosaic. This may take several changes of water.

18 Once the mosaic is dry, a light film of grout residue will appear. Use a combination of slightly damp and clean, dry rags to polish the table.

16 Using the rubber squeegee, spread black grout over the surface, ensuring that all the cracks are filled.

Bathroom splashback

This colourful and whimsical design adds the perfect finishing touch to a bathroom. The mosaic is not laid directly on to the wall but on to a piece of waterproof board, which can be fixed to the wall and easily removed if necessary.

TOOLS

- Pencil
- Ruler
- Stylus (optional)
- Goggles and mask
- Tile nippers
- Mixing containers
- Palette knife
- Rubber gloves
- Rubber squeegee
- Rags or cloths
- Sponges

MATERIALS

- Carbon paper (optional)
- 450 x 600 mm marine plywood or pre-sealed board
- Glass mosaic tesserae: assorted colours (see step 1)
- Coloured glass: green, blue
- Old mirror
- Multi-purpose tile adhesive
- Black grout

PREPARATION
1 This mosaic uses many colours. Using the main photograph as a guide and referring to steps 3–6, choose your own range of colours.

The splashback would work just as well should you prefer to use a less broad range of colours.

2 Enlarge the design, located on page 60, on a photocopier and transfer it on to the splashback using carbon paper and a stylus (see pages 10–12). Alternatively, draw the design directly on to the board.

3 Wearing goggles to protect your eyes, and a mask to prevent inhalation of dust particles, cut enough tesserae for one area of the mosaic.

TILING THE BACKGROUND
4 Start work on the mosaic by outlining the border with blue glass mosaic tesserae. Use rectangular shapes (approximately 20 x 15 mm)

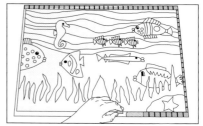

4 Fix thin rectangles down the sides of the border and wider rectangles along the top and bottom.

This splashback uses mainly glass mosaic tesserae, but pieces of mirror and blue and green glass are scattered throughout the design to add areas of interest and contrast.

The fish are quite small and detailed so take care when cutting the tiles so they fit neatly within the drawn lines.

and fix them along the top and bottom. Use thinner rectangles (approximately 20 x 10 mm) and fix them vertically along the two sides.

5 Working from the bottom of the splashback upwards, fill in the seaweed, using three or four shades of green glass mosaic tesserae and pieces of green coloured glass. Add in the sand bank and the orange starfish. Follow the main photograph on page 43 for ideas on colour, or use your own judgement.

Apply the adhesive directly on to the board, but remember that this may obscure your drawn lines. When working on detailed areas, you may find it easier to use the palette knife to butter the back of the individual tessera with the adhesive.

6 The blue background is made up of two shades of light blue and small pieces of blue coloured glass scattered randomly through it.

7 Fill in the waves using various shades of blue and green glass mosaic tesserae. Use blue and green coloured glass and pieces of mirror to make up some of the rows of waves. Alternate the stripes of colour, using the main photograph as a reference.

TILING THE FISH

8 Arrange the tiles for each fish and then butter the backs of the tesserae with adhesive and stick them in place. Use your own judgement and follow the main photograph as a guide when selecting the colours for your fish. Generally, each fish is made up using two or three colours.

The following list is intended as a guide only:

• Fish no. 1: This fish is made up of purple and yellow tesserae. Cut small yellow circles for the fish spots and fix them in place first. Add thin strips of purple and yellow for the fins. Fill in the rest of the body using random

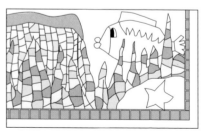

5 Working from the bottom upwards fill in the background using a random pattern of blue toned tesserae.

shapes of purple. Remember to leave room for the eye.

- Fish no. 2: This seahorse is worked using bronze-coloured tesserae. It has a small orange eye.
- Fish no. 3: Outline the fish body using thin, rectangular orange tesserae. Fill in with larger orange tesserae. Use white to fill in the stripe and spots.
- Fish no. 4: These three little fish are quite small and therefore require careful tile cutting to get the exact shapes you need. Use thin yellow strips for the fins, small circles for the eyes, and triangles for the tails. Alternate green and yellow stripes for the body.
- Fish no. 5: Use red tesserae to make up the body of this fish, and add in a small black eye.
- Fish no. 6: Use red tesserae to fill in the stripes and spots for this fish. Fill in the body using green. Use very small pieces of white and black to make up the eye.
- Fish no. 7: Use orange tesserae for the lips, fin and tail, and fill in the body using two shades of purple (see the photograph on page 44). The

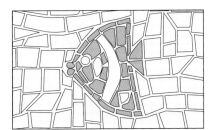

8 Outline the fish (no. 3) with orange tesserae; fill in the body, leaving the areas for the eye, stripe and spots.

BASES FOR WET AREAS

Marine plywood or pre-sealed board are both available from builders' merchants and are good for use in damp areas, such as in bathrooms and kitchens.

---

body of this fish is partially obscured by the seaweed. Fill in the eye with small white and black tessera.

FINISHING

9 Allow 24 hours for the adhesive to dry before grouting with black grout (see Grouting, pages 14–15). Apply the grout with a squeegee or, wearing gloves, use your hands to spread the grout, ensuring it fills all the interstices. Wipe off the excess grout with the squeegee or use a rag.

10 With a damp sponge wipe over the whole surface area to reveal the design. Rinse the sponge out in water as you do this.

11 Once the mosaic is dry, a light film of grout residue will appear. Polish the splashback using a clean, dry rag.

12 Hang the splashback in place (see page 15 for details).

COLOURED GROUT

Instead of purchasing pre-mixed grouts in different colours, add oxides or acrylic paint to dry grout to achieve different colours.

Kitchen splashback

This pretty blue and white splashback is made using a mix of glass mosaic tesserae and, in keeping with the kitchen theme, both plain and patterned broken plates.

TOOLS

- Stylus (optional)
- Ruler
- Pencil
- Tile nippers
- Goggles and mask
- Mixing containers
- Palette knife
- Rubber gloves
- Rubber squeegee
- Rags or cloths
- Sponges

MATERIALS

- Carbon paper (optional)
- 450 x 1200 mm marine plywood or pre-sealed board
- Old blue and white china plates
- Plates or crockery in assorted colours for flowers: yellow, light blue, orange, cornflower blue
- Glass mosaic tesserae: white, blue, turquoise, purple
- White multi-purpose tile adhesive
- White grout

PREPARATION

1 Using a photocopier, enlarge the pattern for the kitchen splashback, located on page 61. Enlarge the pattern as indicated, or to fit the size of your splashback. This pattern repeats itself down the length of the splashback, so duplicate the pattern as many times as needed to fill the length of your splashback. Using carbon paper and the stylus, transfer the design on to the board.

Alternatively, use the pattern as a guide and draw the outline directly on to your board using a ruler and pencil. The following measurements are intended as a guide to help you draw up the design:

- The splashback is 1200 mm long and 450 mm wide.
- The top and bottom borders of the design are made up of 17 squares, with each square measuring approximately 64 x 55 mm.
- The side borders are made up of ten squares measuring approximately 42 x 55 mm (the four corner squares are included here).
- The inner border is tiled with thin purple tesserae and is 10 mm wide.
- Space the crisscrossing lines evenly along the border. There are no exact measurements for these—use your own judgement.
- Draw the flowers within these lines, one in each 'diamond'. All the flowers have ten petals.

Select the colour of your grout carefully as it plays a large part in the overall effect of the mosaic. The white grout used here not only complements the white tesserae but adds to the freshness of the design.

When using white or pale glass mosaic tesserae, it is recommended that you use white adhesive: darker adhesives may be visible through the glass tesserae.

2 To make the crisscrossing lines in the centre of the splashback, cut the blue and white china plates into small squares. Without using any adhesive, lay these out on the design to see if you have enough pieces. When cutting tiles, remember to wear a filter mask to prevent inhalation of dust particles and goggles to protect your eyes .

3 Cut the petals for the six yellow flowers and six light blue circles for the centre of these flowers. Cut small rectangular petals for the five orange flowers and five cornflower blue circles for the centre of these flowers.

4 The centre of the design is worked using random shapes of white glass mosaic tesserae. The border of the splashback uses rectangular and triangular shapes of blue, turquoise and purple glass mosaic tesserae. Cut these tesserae now or, if preferred, cut them as needed.

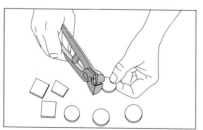

3 Cut the centres for the flowers: use the tile nippers to shape the small squares of crockery into circles.

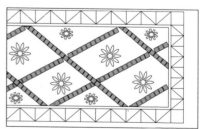

5 Spread the adhesive on the back of the individual pieces of tesserae and place them along the drawn lines.

FIXING THE TESSERAE

5 Using white adhesive, fix the blue and white china pieces to form the crisscrosses. You may want to butter the backs of the tesserae with the adhesive so the design lines remain visible as you work. If you apply the adhesive directly to the surface, you will cover these lines, and will then need to work carefully to keep the lines as straight as possible.

6 Add in the yellow and orange flowers. Position the round tesserae for the centre of the flower first and then add the petals. To ensure the petals are well-balanced, first lay out the petals around the flower before fixing them permanently in place with adhesive.

7 Complete the centre of the design using white tesserae. Use small wedge-shaped pieces to fill in the spaces around the petals.

8 Cut the purple glass mosaic tesserae into thin rectangles, approximately 20 x 10 mm, and stick them in a single row around the white tesserae.

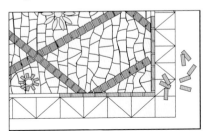

8 Butter the backs of the purple glass tesserae and position them as a border running around the central design.

> **CAUTION**
>
> Be aware that if you use crockery in your mosaic, the uneven surface of the pieces may jut out slightly. Take care when wiping over the splashback with a cloth so the rough edges do not catch the cloth or scratch you.
>
> For a completely smooth surface, replace the crockery with glass mosaic tesserae, or patterned tiles that are the same thickness as the other materials used.

9 Fill in the corners of the splashback with purple tesserae. The rest of the border is made up of triangles of turquoise and blue.

FINISHING

10 Allow 24 hours for the adhesive to dry before grouting with white grout. Using the rubber squeegee, apply liberal amounts of the grout over the surface, pushing it into all the cracks. Alternatively, as the surface is a little uneven, it may be easier to spread the grout with your hands (wearing rubber gloves). Wipe off the excess with a cloth or rag.

11 With a damp sponge, wipe over the surface to remove the grout and to reveal the design. Rinse the sponge out in water several times to ensure all the grout is removed.

12 Once the mosaic is dry, a light film of grout will appear. Polish the surface using a clean, dry rag.

Birdbath

Larger projects, such as this colourful birdbath, may take two or three sittings to complete. The actual design is quite simple: what really makes this birdbath so effective is the use of bright colour and the varying angles at which the tesserae are laid.

TOOLS

- Brush for sealer
- Pencil
- Compass
- Stylus (optional)
- Tile nippers
- Goggles and mask
- Mixing containers
- Palette knife
- Rubber gloves
- Rubber squeegee
- Rags or cloths
- Sponges

MATERIALS

- Concrete birdbath (with dish and stand in separate pieces)
- Waterproof sealer for concrete
- Cement-based tile adhesive
- Old china or crockery: assorted patterns
- Glass mosaic tesserae: yellow, purple, red, light blue, bronze, turquoise, dark blue
- Black grout

PREPARATION

1 Seal all the surfaces of the birdbath (both sides of the dish and the stand) with concrete waterproofing sealer and allow it to dry.

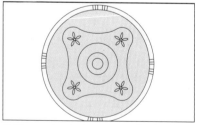

2 Draw the design on to the birdbath using a pencil. Draw three circles, the floral shape and the four flowers.

2 As the design for the birdbath contains little detail, follow the illustration below and draw the design directly on to the birdbath. Start by locating the centre of the birdbath and draw three circles approximately 20 mm, 30 mm and 65 mm in diameter. You can use a compass to do this or a string and pencil (see page 39).

Add in the large floral shape around the outer circle, and the four small flowers in each of the corners. Draw in the detail on the four areas around the rim.

You do not need to draw a pattern for the birdbath stand as the design is worked to suit the shape of your particular stand.

When selecting your birdbath, choose one that is simple in design with as many smooth surfaces as possible. Too many curves and raised patterns will cause difficulties when you are trying to fix the tesserae in place.

The contours of your stand will determine the best way to mosaic it. Follow the photograph as a guide for tiling your own stand.

TILING THE DISH

3 Start working in the centre of the birdbath. Using tile nippers, cut a small circle from the patterned china. Fix it in the centre using adhesive. Surround this with a border of china tesserae to complete the first circle.

4 Add a row of yellow to complete the second circle.

5 Cut the purple tesserae into thin rectangular shapes and lay them around the yellow circle, radiating outwards. Surround this with a border of red and then light blue to complete the third circle.

6 Cut four small circles from the crockery and fix them in the centre

of each flower. For each flower, cut five petal shapes from the bronze tesserae. Butter the back of the tesserae with adhesive and fix in place.

7 Define the large floral shape by outlining it with thin rectangles of turquoise. Fill inside this area with random shapes of turquoise and outline with a row of yellow.

8 Place a row of thin rectangles of dark blue around the yellow. Fill in the remaining area on the dish using randomly shaped blue tesserae.

9 Stick a row of whole blue tesserae around the inside rim. Apply the adhesive with a palette knife and allow it to dry for 10 minutes so the adhesive becomes slightly tacky. If it is wet, the tesserae will slide down the side. Position the uncut edge of the tesserae uppermost to make the finish neater. Allow the adhesive to set.

10 Turn the dish over and tile the back. Starting in the centre, stick a row of thin, red tesserae around the dish, followed by a row of light blue.

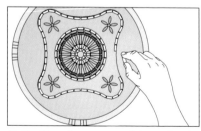

7 Outline the outer and inner border of the floral shape using rectangular turquoise tesserae.

Fill in with turquoise. The outside rim is tiled with purple. Allow to dry before turning it face up.

11 Tile the top of the rim. Start with the four detailed areas. Cut four small squares from crockery and fix them in place. Border these with red, then yellow tesserae cut into thin rectangles. Fill in around the rim with light blue tesserae.

TILING THE STAND
12 Cut the flowers from pieces of china and stick them randomly around the main section of the stand.

13 Fill in around the flowers using dark blue. Tile the rest of the stand using the photograph on the left as a guide. You may need to alter the tiling pattern slightly, depending on the size and shape of your stand.

FINISHING
14 Allow 24 hours for the adhesive to dry. Wearing gloves, spread the black grout over the surface of the birdbath. Wipe off the excess with a rag (see Grouting, pages 14–15).

Do not forget to mosaic the back of the dish. Choose two or three colours and fix them in bands on the back.

15 Allow the grout to dry; turn the dish over and repeat the process to grout the back. While the dish is drying, grout the stand.

16 Once dry, give the birdbath a final polish with a rag to remove any grout residue. Allow at least 72 hours for curing before using the birdbath.

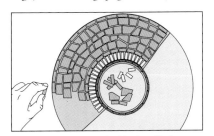

10 Working on half the dish at a time, apply the tesserae to the back of the dish.

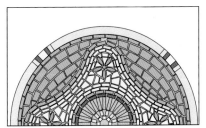

11 Use small squares of crockery and red and yellow tesserae and place them on four points around the rim.

Add impact to an area of plain tiling with this feature mosaic floor panel. Remember to check that the depth of the inset is the same as the depth of tiles (or other flooring material that you intend to use) so the finished floor is level.

Floor inset

This floor inset is made using the indirect method of applying mosaics. The tesserae are glued face down on a piece of brown paper and, when completed, transferred on to a waterproof board, which is inserted into the floor. This method ensures the surface of the inset is perfectly level.

TOOLS

- Stylus (optional)
- Pencil
- Ruler
- Felt-tipped pen
- Goggles and mask
- Tile nippers
- Mixing containers
- Brush
- Rubber gloves
- Palette knife
- Small trowel
- Rubber squeegee
- Sponges
- Rags or cloths

MATERIALS

- Carbon paper (optional)
- 700 x 700 mm brown paper or craft paper
- 50 x 50 mm glass mosaic tesserae: cream, light green
- 20 x 20 mm glass mosaic tesserae: dark brown, maroon, cream, yellow, black, dark orange, caramel
- Wallpaper paste
- Multi-purpose tile adhesive
- 600 x 600 mm marine plywood or pre-sealed board (see Hint, page 45)

PREPARATION

1 Using a photocopier increase the the pattern for the floor inset to the correct size (see page 62). Transfer the design on to a piece of brown paper using carbon paper and the stylus. If the pencilled lines are difficult to see on the brown paper, draw over them with a felt-tipped pen.

The design is 600 x 600 mm, but cut the brown paper larger than this so it is easier to handle when you have to transfer the tesserae off the paper on to the waterproof board.

Alternatively, as this is quite a basic design, you may find it easier to draw the design on the brown paper using a pencil and ruler, following the measurements on the pattern. Add in the flower motifs by hand.

2 Wearing goggles and a mask, cut enough tesserae to start work on one area. Start with the four green and white bands. These bands are made up of whole, large cream tesserae and light green tesserae, which are cut in half diagonally to form two triangles.

3 Following the manufacturer's directions, prepare a small amount of wallpaper paste.

FIXING THE TESSERAE

4 Using a brush, apply wallpaper paste to the brown paper, along one of the bands. Lay the uncut cream tesserae first, placing them upside down on the glue. Similarly, fix the half green tesserae in place. Complete all the bands in this manner.

5 Add crisscrossing lines of thin brown tesserae around these tiles. Remember to lay all the tiles upside down. Place a small maroon square at the point where the lines intersect.

6 Work on the central large flower. Using tile nippers, cut a circle from a small cream tessera and place it in the centre of the flower. Add a row of thin rectangular tesserae outlining the circle. Border this with a row of maroon. Fill in the petals with yellow.

7 Outline the black square with a border of thin, rectangular black tesserae. Fill in the area around the

yellow flower with randomly shaped pieces of black.

8 Add two rows of smaller cream tesserae around the black square. These tesserae are used whole. To each corner add an uncut dark orange tessera outlined by a border of black.

9 Fill in the four flowers on the outer corners with dark orange, and fill in the remaining area of the square with black.

10 Outline the cream and green bands with a single row of thin maroon tesserae. Fill in the outer border with caramel, worked in a basketweave pattern (see the photograph on the right).

11 When the design is completed, allow the wallpaper adhesive to dry for 24 hours before transferring the tesserae to the waterproof board.

TRANSFERRING THE TESSERAE

12 Using a trowel, apply a thin, even bed of adhesive to the board.

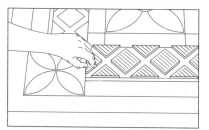

4 Apply wallpaper paste to one area at a time and place the tesserae upside down on the brown paper.

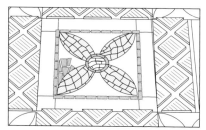

7 Position a row of black tesserae around the border of the square; fill in the remaining area.

The edge of the inset is made up of a row of maroon, and a basketweave pattern made up of caramel tesserae.

13 Working quickly (but carefully) so that the adhesive does not dry out, lift the tiled design on the brown paper and turn it over on to the waterproof board, aligning the edges of the tiled design with the board. The back of the tesserae should be sitting in the adhesive and the brown paper should be facing upwards. Ensure the tiles are pressed evenly into the bed of adhesive. Allow the adhesive to dry for 24 hours.

14 Using a damp sponge and warm water, dampen the surface of the paper. The paper will easily peel off the surface of the mosaic to reveal the design, right way up.

FINISHING

15 Using the rubber squeegee, apply the grey grout over the surface (see pages 14–15). Wipe off the excess with the squeegee or use a cloth.

16 With a damp sponge, and rinsing regularly, wipe off the excess grout. When dry, polish the surface using a clean rag.

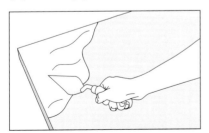

12 Using a small trowel, apply a thin bed of tile adhesive to the waterproof board.

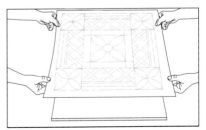

13 Lift the tesserae on the brown paper and place it on to the board with the paper facing upwards.

Patterns

Fruit bowl (page 28)

Using a photocopier, enlarge each image by 250% (enlarge by 200%, and then by 125%).

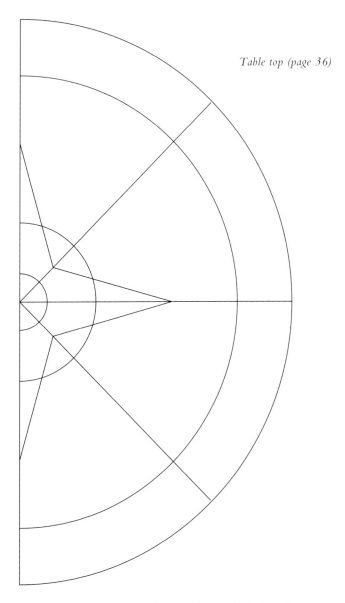

Table top (page 36)

Using a photocopier, enlarge the image by 666% (enlarge by
200%, then 200%, and then by 167%). Reverse the
pattern for the other half of the table.

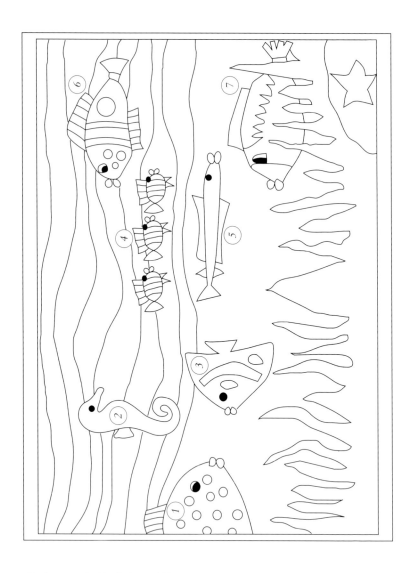

Bathroom splashback (page 42)

Using a photocopier, enlarge the image by 444% (enlarge by 200%, then 200%, and then by 111%).

Kitchen splashback (page 46)

Using a photocopier, enlarge the image by 500% (enlarge by 200%, then 200%, and then by 125%).

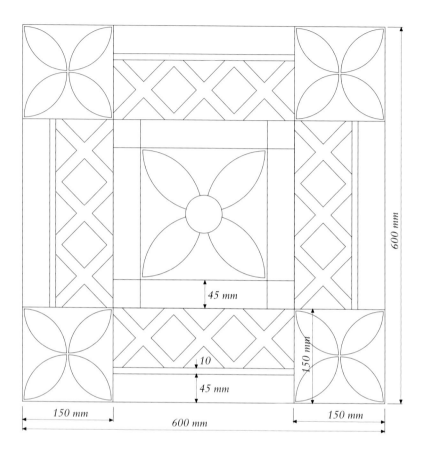

Floor inset (page 54)

Using a photocopier, enlarge the image by 600% (enlarge by 200%, then 200%, and then by 150%).

Tools for making mosaics

You do not need many tools to complete a mosaic project, and most of what you need can be found around the home. Your local hardware store will also stock most of these items.

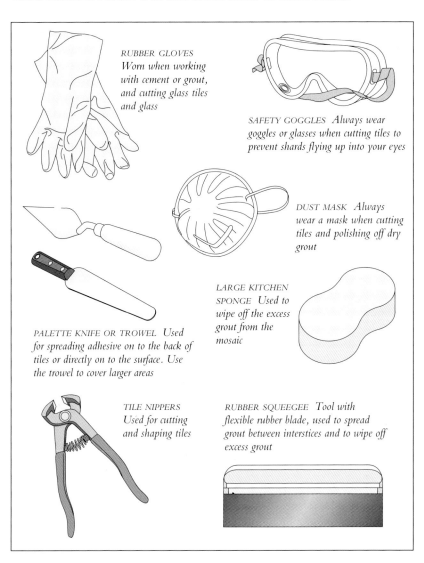

RUBBER GLOVES *Worn when working with cement or grout, and cutting glass tiles and glass*

SAFETY GOGGLES *Always wear goggles or glasses when cutting tiles to prevent shards flying up into your eyes*

DUST MASK *Always wear a mask when cutting tiles and polishing off dry grout*

LARGE KITCHEN SPONGE *Used to wipe off the excess grout from the mosaic*

PALETTE KNIFE OR TROWEL *Used for spreading adhesive on to the back of tiles or directly on to the surface. Use the trowel to cover larger areas*

TILE NIPPERS *Used for cutting and shaping tiles*

RUBBER SQUEEGEE *Tool with flexible rubber blade, used to spread grout between interstices and to wipe off excess grout*

Index